*"To the leopard and the Mumbaikar, may our forests flourish and provide for both."*
- **Lubaina Bandukwala**

*"For my daughter, Duniya."*
- **Allen Shaw**

Third reprint February 2026
Text: Lubaina Bandukwala
Illustrations: Allen Shaw

Karadi Tales Company Pvt. Ltd.
3A, Dev Regency, 11, First Main Road,
Gandhi Nagar, Adyar, Chennai - 600020
Tel: +91-44-42054243
Email: contact@karaditales.com
Website: www.karaditales.com
ISBN: 978-81-939033-4-6

Printed by Quarterfold
Printabilities Private Limited

**Leopard in Mumbai**

# Leopard in Mumbai

Lubaina Bandukwala
Allen Shaw

This morning, I stepped out from
Sanjay Gandhi National Park.

I caught a fast train from Borivali to Bandra.
Everyone in my compartment quickly cleared out.

How bizarre!

I wandered into a school with colourful toys
where children pointed at me joyfully.
The adults did not look as happy.

How baffling!

At the Mount Mary Church Festival,
I wanted a toy. But the shopkeeper
refused to come down from the roof.

How strange!

TOYS

I slipped into a taxi that flew over the grand Bandra-Worli Sea Link. But the driver took one good look at me and fled!

How funny!

FOR HIRE
MH LEO 710
MH LEO 710

I curled up on top of a big red bus.

From my perch, I saw the Haji Ali Mosque
in the middle of the sea, the Babulnath temple,
and Chowpatty beach.

I leaned down to ask the driver to stop - and
suddenly it was utter chaos!

How peculiar!

बेस्ट

I stepped over to the bhel puri stall, helped myself to some bhel puri and pav bhaaji, and took a bite of vada pav too, while taking in the view of Marine Drive.

H/W
L.C.No.9

I jumped into an open truck and found myself driving past the Horniman Circle and the Asiatic library.

MH-LEO
2213

The truck finally stopped right where I wanted - the Gateway of India.

*Mumbai, I have arrived,* I thought.

MH-LEO
2213

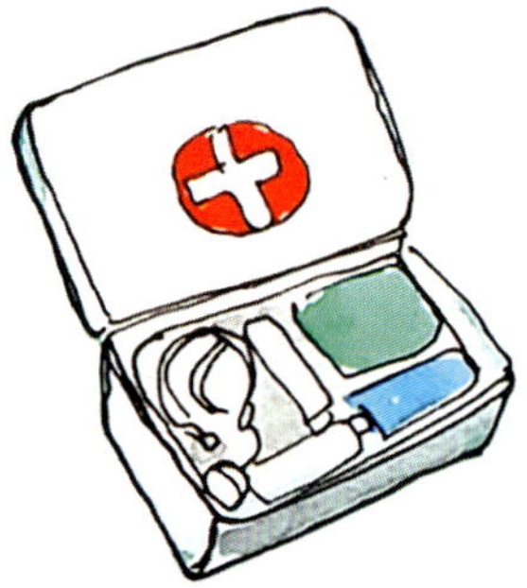

All of a sudden, everything went black.

Next thing I knew, I was back in the leafy green Sanjay Gandhi National Park, looking at the beautiful Kanheri Caves.

Did I really have a Mumbai adventure?
Or was it a dream?

I raised my paw to scratch my face and caught a whiff of pav bhaaji.

Hmm . . . probably not!

Mumbai
MUMBAI
BORIVALI
PAW
LEO

E
N
S
W

## A City of Diverse Inhabitants

Today, over 20 million people call the city of Mumbai home. But long before it became the bustling metropolis it is, Mumbai used to be an archipelago of seven islands. The area was ruled by many different empires over the centuries, including the British, the Portuguese, the Gujarat Sultanate, the Shilaharas, and the Satavahanas. In the third century BCE (over 2300 years ago!), it was a part of the Maurya empire, ruled by the emperor Ashoka. During his reign, the Buddhist monuments known as the Kanheri Caves were carved in what is today the Sanjay Gandhi National Park.

Before any of these empires ruled Mumbai, however, it was home to the Koli fishing community, whose goddess Mumbadevi lends her name to the city.

And all along, through all of this history, the people of Mumbai have lived alongside the original Mumbaikars: a wide range of wildlife including birds, butterflies, monkeys, crocodiles, deer, and, of course, leopards. Today, many of these animals live in the Sanjay Gandhi National Park, a forested area in the northern suburbs of Mumbai.

As of 2020, over 45 leopards live in the park and, much like humans, leopards are tremendously adaptable. They hunt and survive in a wide range of environments including rainforests, steppes, and even cities. Leopards tend to be reclusive creatures, stalking their prey and hunting under the cover of night. As the areas around the Sanjay Gandhi National Park have become more densely populated, the leopards of Mumbai do occasionally encounter humans – in fact, this very book is based on a couple of true incidents that have occurred in the city!

If you do see a leopard in the city, stay calm, keep your distance and call for help!

## Glossary

**Bhel puri:** A much-loved savoury snack made of puffed rice, vegetables and tamarind sauce.

**Pav bhaaji:** A street-food item that consists of red vegetable curry served with buns.

**Vada pav:** A fast-food dish that consists of a deep-fried potato patty served inside a bun.

## Places

### Sanjay Gandhi National Park:

Sanjay Gandhi National Park, which Leopard strolls out of, is an 87 kilometer-long stretch of protected land in Mumbai. It is the only protected forest in the country that lies in a metropolis. The park is said to be home to 274 species of birds, 35 species of mammals, 170 species of butterflies and over 1300 species of trees.

Inside the forests of Sanjay Gandhi National Park lies the ancient Kanheri Caves. These caves contain Buddhist carvings, paintings, and inscriptions dating back to the 1st century, and are witness to the handiwork of Ashoka's daughter who brought Buddhism to Nala Sopara en route to Sri Lanka.

### Borivali Railway Station:

Slow, semi-fast, and fast trains (the last of which Leopard took to Bandra) all stop at the Borivali Railway Station. Mumbai's incredibly expansive network of suburban trains was the very first railway network to be built in all of Asia (in use since 1853). Every day, the trains are used by approximately 7.5 million people, and the remarkable frequency at which these trains arrive allows for this. The most iconic of Mumbai's train stations is the Chhatrapati Shivaji Terminus.

### Mount Mary Church:

Situated on a hillock overlooking the Arabian sea, Mount Mary Church was constructed in the 16th century by Portuguese priests who brought with them a statue of Mother Mary during the Portuguese occupation of Mumbai.

The Mount Mary Church Festival that Leopard attends is a week-long fair held in Bandra which takes place every year starting on the Sunday following 8th September. It attracts thousands of visitors annually, and is filled with stalls selling food, candles, and religious objects.

### Bandra-Worli Sea Link:

There cannot be mention of Mumbai without a mention of the iconic Bandra-Worli sea link, so distinctive to Mumbai's landscape, which is a bridge that runs over the ocean connecting Bandra (which is in the Western Suburbs of Mumbai) with Worli (which is in the South of Mumbai).

### Haji Ali Mosque:

The Haji Ali Mosque that Leopard views atop a double-decker bus, quite literally appears to float in the middle of the sea. Built in the 19th century, the mosque also contains the tomb of Pir Haji Ali Shah Bukhari, a Sufi saint.

The hall of the mosque is known for its exquisite marble pillars that are embellished with intricate multi-coloured mirror-work.

### Babulnath Temple:

One of the oldest temples in Mumbai, Babulnath Temple is a temple dedicated to the Hindu god Shiva. It dates back to the 12th century when the temple was consecrated by Raja Bhimdev who was the king of the region at the time.

It remains a popular tourist spot to this day. The snacks - known locally as farsan - sold in the shops outside the temple are a much-loved delicacy.

### Marine Drive:

Marine drive is a promenade that stretches for 3.9 kms along the Netaji Subhash Chandra Bose Road. Its C shape, and the fact that it is dotted with street-lights along its edge, has earned it the name 'Queen's Necklace'. At the northern end of Marine drive is Chowpatty Beach, another location Leopard visits.

### Horniman Circle and the Asiatic Library:

Horniman Circle is a large garden covering an area of around 12,081 square yards in South Mumbai. It is named for Benjamin Horniman, the British editor of *The Bombay Chronicle*, who was a supporter of India's Independence movement. The garden, which is an important landmark in Mumbai, has earned the name 'City Green' and is the spot from where distances in Mumbai are measured. For instance, a milestone that says 'Mumbai, 45 kms' is measuring the distance from Horniman Circle to that milestone.

Overlooking Horniman Circle is Mumbai's Asiatic Library, a majestic structure that houses the Asiatic Society of Bombay, a public library, a fantastic resource of information on literature, science, and the oriental arts.

### Gateway of India:

In 1911, King George V landed in Mumbai and, to commemorate the visit of the first British monarch to land on Indian shores, the Gateway of India was built. Not only is it a symbol to represent British colonisers entering India, it is also from where the last of the British troops left India in 1948, after India had gained independence.